T·H·E
CRUCIAL
QUESTIONS

T·H·E
CRUCIAL QUESTIONS

A New Age Approach to Self-Discovery

Lawrence M. Steinhart

THE
DONNING COMPANY
PUBLISHERS
NORFOLK/VIRGINIA BEACH

This book is dedicated to life—and the many wonderful friends who have enriched mine. They have helped me formulate the questions both intentionally and unintentionally. They know who they are—and I would like to take this opportunity of acknowledging them and reaffirming my love for them.

Copyright © 1989 by Lawrence Steinhart

All rights reserved, including the right to reproduce this work in any form whatsoever without permission in writing from the publisher, except for brief passages in connection with a review. For information, write:

The Donning Company/Publishers
5659 Virginia Beach Boulevard
Norfolk, Virginia 23502

Library of Congress Cataloging-in-Publication Data

Steinhart, Lawrence M.
 The crucial questions.
 1. Self-actualization (Psychology)—Problems, exercises,
etc. 2 Self-perception—Problems, exercises,
etc. 3. Self-evaluation. 4. New Age movements.
I. Title.
BG637.S4S79 1989 131 88-33498
ISBN 0-89865-719-9

Printed in the United States of America

Table of Contents

Preface 7
To Start At The Very Beginning 19
Personal Image 21
Personal Relationships 25
Family Relations 29
Business Relations 31
On Wealth (or Lack Of) 33
Addictions 35
On Health and Healing 37
On Sexuality 41
On Death and Dying 45
Reincarnation—Other Lives 49
God, Saints and Devils 51
Universal Philosophy 55
Dreams 59
Attitudinal Responses 61
Beliefs, Programs and Mundanities 65
Futures 67
Epilogue 69

Preface

In 1971, I left a lucrative career in New York to go to Virginia Beach. It was a sudden decision, but the result of an increased dissatisfaction with values which had been previously accepted without question. What ensued was tantamount to a spiritual odyssey.

It started through an invitation by the late Hugh Lynn Cayce, son of Edgar Cayce, the famed seer of Virginia Beach—the Sleeping Prophet—to write a book on health and beauty based on the information which his father had channeled while in trance.[1] Edgar Cayce has been considered by many to be the father of the wholistic health movement which is gaining momentum in the world today.

The difference between modern medicine and wholism is that one often treats only symptoms and their immediate causes while the other attempts to get right down to the root cause, start the healing process there while alleviating the discomfort arising from external symptoms. Wholism, while treating the physical body recognizes that a pain in one location can originate in a completely different area of the body. It also

[1] *Edgar Cayce's Secrets of Beauty Through Health*

attempts to bring the physical into alignment with the mental and spiritual bodies.

Some years ago, the term "psychosomatic illness" became popular. It was a term used to sweep every malaise which could not be explained by modern science under a convenient mat. Today, in the framework of wholistic concepts, it seems that everything is psychosomatically induced. Edgar Cayce used the phrase "mind is the builder" so many times in his readings that it has become a catch phrase with people familiar with them. However, the really deep and enduring message behind this phrase needs to sink gradually into our consciousness before it can be recognized in its entirety. The Reverend Norman Vincent Peale first popularized the term "positive thinking" and attributed power to it. The scriptures acknowledge the power of the mind by admitting that "as a man thinketh...." This concept is not, for some, a very comfortable one. It throws all responsibility for anything which may happen back onto the individual. We cannot blame a bacteria or virus for attacking us and causing a sickness. Falls and other accidents cannot be the root cause of problems; they might be the immediate cause, but what led up to the accident and why did we attract the situation?

This book is designed to be non-invasive; a totally cooperative venture between its author and reader—me and you. Its size may belie its profound message and potential impact. It is designed to be read, not once and then passed over and put aside, but monthly, quarterly or whenever. Time should be put aside to allow reflection on the questions. Write down the answers in a notebook, restating the question if necessary so that your answer will read as a complete statement—I find that each time I go through the book, the self-portrait which emerges will change. I know when it is time to re-sculpt my personal portrait when I read over my notebook from the last entries and find that I do not agree with some of my own statements. It is surprising how frequently and how quickly my "truisms" change. How often and how much we change is entirely dependent on the energy we focus on personal growth. Only you can decide what kind of changes you want to make, if any, and how this book can best serve your needs.

There are no right or wrong answers to **any** of the questions. However, it is not always easy for me to resist the temptation to judge myself on the responses or the answers. The sole object is to be able to look at oneself objectively—recognize the boundaries we have chosen, then expand them, accept them, or tear them down as we see fit. What we get will be a picture of the world according to us.

Working With Research of Psychic Diagnosticians

Part of my personal growth experience was due to

the time I spent "conducting" trance psychics. This work was done in the spirit of research in "wholistic" health. It was during this time that the real meaning of "**MIND IS THE BUILDER**" started to sink in.

When the psychic diagnostician went into trance, a conductor was needed, that is, someone who would act as an anchor between the psychic, travelling in the outer reaches of consciousness, and the here-and-now. If the patient were present during the reading, I would sit between them to prevent anyone touching or disturbing the psychic while in trance. When the reading was over, many of the terms, instructions, and explanations used by the psychic were strange to the patient, and as the psychic was virtually absent during the reading, he or she had no recollection of what was said. It was my job then to interpret what transpired, clear up any misunderstandings and clarify what, if anything, needed to be done.

One of the tools with which psychics like to work are questions formulated by the recipient of the reading or discourse. These questions help the psychic to tune into the level of consciousness of the individual. For one wanting to know about the state of his or her health, it matters little if the psychic discourses on rays, planes, or other esoteric intangibles. Or, if the concern uppermost in the mind concerns business or finances, advice on nutrition does not always fall on friendly ears. In the asking of the questions, the psychic can tune in and give the information needed. Realizing the importance of balancing all aspects of the individual, the psychic can then branch off into another aspect which will affect the total person. This information will then fall on more receptive ears when the prime questions are answered.

I have been told that Gertrude Stein, on her deathbed, was asked if she knew the answer to life, to which she replied, "What is the question?" Often individuals find trouble in formulating questions. It seems that everyone knows the answers, but few know which questions to ask. This book asks the questions which will help us, if we will take the time to work with them to discover the inner image of ourselves which we are accepting. This image is not always the one we want. Sometimes it is downright painful, but necessary to recognize if we want to change—or learn to love ourselves. It should become less painful each time we play the "answer game" if we are serious about working with ourselves—or even just watching our evolution with an objective eye.

Psychoanalysis can cover a period of years and cost hundreds or thousands of dollars—not counting the time involved lying on a couch (or whatever process is in vogue at the moment). Maybe the length of time is needed just to open up to another person. No matter how much we trust and love another, there are certain parts of ourselves which we are reluctant to share. The mere fact that another is present while we are evaluating ourselves can be sufficient cause for us to raise automatic defenses. Our innate desire to please (as an approval getter) might engender responses which are what we believe our therapist would like to hear—or what we would like our therapist to hear—regardless of how far it might be from the truth. Therapy can also become a crutch, an addiction. Therapy dependence can be a trap which we may fall into all too easily. In therapy, we work towards a goal—but how do we know when we have reached that goal? If being comfortable is the goal, who determines when that comfort level is reached and we might well ask the question, "Is anyone ever really comfortable?" If we go into therapy because we are organically or severely mentally ill the decision about the time to leave therapy is an easy one, when we are once again able to function within the framework of society. But if the issue is one of confidence or self esteem, the decision to leave is more difficult. Do we ever feel that we have fully reached the expectations we set for ourselves? Working within **this** format, using THE CRUCIAL QUESTIONS, would be a very valuable personal and private psychoanalysis.

Group Work

Although *The Crucial Questions* was not designed to be studied as a group effort, I can see the value of it as an alternative study method. The highest quality personal growth occurs when we can go within to the ultimate teacher—our own inner voice, but this contact is not always made. For those of us who need feedback and support, the group experience is ideal.

We are all too often inclined to think that our own belief structure is the norm or that which is generally accepted by the majority of the populace. It is not until we really get together with others and explore these beliefs that we realize how **truly** individual we all are. There are no two people exactly alike. In spite of these differences we live in a homogenous world but it is the acceptance of everyone else's beliefs—and the acceptance of their wishes—that creates the peaceful environment toward which many of us strive.

Plumbing our depths alone and in private can work for some. Others may not have the personal discipline to succeed or may not have the strength to really be truthful with themselves. Some of us may not even recognize the truth, having told ourselves a story which glosses over the truth for so long that we have actually grown to believe it.

Group therapy can be a most effective tool. Group work requires truthfulness. Maintaining a lie is not easy, especially when there is an attentively listening group of people. It is very likely that sooner or later someone in the group will confront the lie. If the group accepted our lies, they would not be truly loving or supportive. After all, personal growth is the object of time spent together, and if we are not serious about it, it is a waste not only of our time but that of the group also. At first, we might find it difficult to reveal ourself (self-disclosure) in front of others, but after we do and we find the environment one of trust, it could become a highly stimulating experience which will give us a "high" that can last for days. It can take time to feel safe in a group environment before self-disclosure comes easily (if it ever does), therefore the selection process in choosing a group is most important.

Although this book can be used as a group activity—and I foresee this as a distinct possibility—its prime value lies in the fact that it can be worked with alone, in the privacy of our own home. As our responses are not designed to impress another, they are more likely to be honest responses.

The Changing Universe

The Crucial Questions is not designed to be read through in an evening as one would read a story. It is designed rather to stimulate our minds—something to be experienced. If you decide to spend an evening just contemplating the first page or even the first question—that's okay. Being told the answer to a question rarely implants the information into our consciousness. If the answers we are seeking are profound (or profoundly important to us), finding them for ourselves will give the information far greater meaning. The word "education" comes from the Latin *e* + *ducere* and its meaning is to bring out the knowledge from deep within. This assumes that everyone contains all knowledge, all answers. However, if we are given the answer by another, it is **their** answer, not ours. Eliciting a response from within by questioning implants the information into our memory banks. Being given an answer does not always mean that it will take root. With so much emphasis being placed on the exploration of outer space, let us create a balance by placing our personal emphasis on **inner space**, a subject about which probably less is known than outer space.

Perhaps the only revelation that might come out of this book is in showing the depth of conviction we have in our own beliefs. Why have we such a deep conviction? It might depend on any one of a number of reasons. It could come from a deep inner knowing—an instinct—or it might come from our teaching or programming. Perhaps it comes from the need to be "in the know," the "connoisseur syndrome." Sometimes we need to "know" all the answers to save face, or maybe we believe that not knowing the answer might detract from our personal charisma giving us a sense of helplessness. Very often, just saying "I don't know" can be traumatic for us. Ask directions of people in the street and watch the reactions of those who do not know the answer. Scripture tells us that fear of the Lord is the beginning of wisdom. The beginning of wisdom could also be facing the unknown without fear (well, maybe just a little trepidation).

Questioning ourself can be a very hard discipline, especially if we patiently wait for the answers to formulate themselves. Sometimes we plough through a list of questions as though we were filling in an application form for a mortgage, or some other task we want to complete as quickly as possible—a feat, a chore, just one more responsibility in the game of life. Coming up with honest answers might well be traumatic.

To say that many of these questions are not mine personally would be a lie. They have very often burrowed inside of me. They could not be escaped. I have often questioned whether others go through this self-searching—and if they did, what answers did they come up with? And if they didn't, why didn't they? Do the answers really matter or is the attitude we live with more important than knowing the whys and wherefores of life?

One "truism" (for me) that I keep returning to is that our personal life situations do not matter. The decision to do this, that, or the other thing, which seems so important at the time, is not the matter of prime importance. There is not a right or wrong decision. One decision merely brings one set of circumstances in its wake and another a different set. What **is** of prime importance is the attitude with which we face the circumstances, be they pleasant or less than pleasant. The attitude which I have found to bring me the most peace is an attitude of gratitude. What often seems today like a major catastrophe can appear tomorrow as a blessing when we can look back on the whole blueprint. As the old saying goes: Hindsight has twenty-twenty vision.

The only constant in the universe is change. Consequently, when we view our self-portrait, merely view it—let's not judge it. If there are things we see which we would rather not see, we can replace them with those characteristics which we would prefer.

If we reach a point where we are happy with what we see, revel in it, bask in it, but do not expect the status quo to remain. The universe is in a constant state of "becoming" and to expect to find completion is really not possible. As soon as we find it, within that moment it is starting its change. There *is* perfection "in the present moment," but we have to live in that holy instant, slipping out of it for just a second can bring discomfort. If we slip into the past, we risk experiencing guilt. If we look to the future, we risk anxiety. Peace is most easily found in the present moment.

To Start at the Very Beginning

Was my parents' pregnancy with me a planned one?

Do (or did) I know my parents?

Did my parents really want me?
   Was I the sex that they had hoped for?
   Does my name reflect the opposite sex?

What was my parents' financial status at the time of my birth?

Was my birth a simple, uncomplicated one?
   If not, does (or did) my mother ever refer to it?

Are my memories of childhood filled with parental love?

Was I attended by a nurse or one other than my parents?

Do my memories of childhood include recall of abuse, overstrict or uncaring parents?

What is the earliest recall I have of my parents?

Do I feel comfortable with the family into which I was born?

Personal Image

Who am I?

Which ten adjectives do I feel sincerely describe me as I see and know me.

Which ten adjectives do I feel my close friends would use to describe me.

What image do I have of myself?
   How do I look?
   What do my clothes lend to my appearance?
     Do they enhance or detract from the image I would like?
     Or are they unimportant?
   Am I underweight? Overweight? Just right?
   Am I overdeveloped? Underdeveloped? Just right?
   Am I in "good shape?"
   What would be needed to put me into my ideal condition?

Am I:
   Loving? Within the home situation? Within my immediate circle of friends? With everyone? or,

Am I aloof—detached?
Fearful? If yes:
Is my fear an abstract? Or can I name it?
Do I fear?
   Sickness
   Death
   Old age
   Being alone
   Being responsible for someone's happiness?
   Dependence (lack of work, home, money, etc.)
   Other's opinions
   Judgements—my own or others'
   Confrontations
   The law
   Demanding what is rightfully mine
   Telling bad news
   Refusing a request
   Underlining a painful truth
   Being loved
   Rejection
   Include any pet fears I may have here and make note of them to work on at a later time.

Am I?
   Vengeful
   Spiteful (after being slighted—imagined or real)
   Helpful

Accommodating
Always on the fence
Always on the defense
Am I hostile (if so how frequently—or always)?
Do I make decisions without a great deal of effort?
Do I have trouble making decisions—do I procrastinate?

How often do I use the expression "I ought to," "I need to," or "I should" instead of "I WANT TO" or "I WILL"?

What percentage of the day do I devote to worrying?

What alternatives are there to worrying?

Should something go wrong, how do I handle it?
What is my attitude?

In conversation:
Do I question others? How attentively do I listen to the answers?
Do I wait to interject a personal experience relating to the subject under discussion...or even change to a completely different subject?
Do I reveal my experiences since our last meeting?

How often do I slip into the mode of saying, "If only—or what if?"

Am I at peace with the image of myself that I have created?

If not:
How would I like to see myself?
What can I do to implement the changes?

Do I have a hero/heroine to whom I look up?
Do I have an anti-hero/anti-heroine?
Are there any parts of me that are similar or parallel to either of these?

A great poet/writer/thinker once said that all the world's a stage and we are merely players. Do I believe this is true?
What role am I playing in this cosmic drama?
Is it a starring role? a supporting role? or just an extra?
Am I happy with the status of my role?

"If a man does not keep pace with his companions, perhaps it is because he hears a different drummer..."
                                    Thoreau

Do I keep pace with my companions?
Do I hear a different drummer?

Personal Relationships

Do I believe that there is a soulmate "out there"—one perfect soul of which I am the exact match, or counterpart?
  Do I need that other soul for me to be a whole unit?

On what do I found a primary one-on-one relationship?
  What is the most important aspect of the relationship?

In which role do I see myself in this relationship?
  Am I content to be in this role?
    If not, which role would I prefer it to be?

In which role do I see my mate?
  Do I think that he/she is content in this role?
  What role do I think he/she wishes to be in?
  Could I play off that role?

In which role do I think my mate sees me?

What percentage of the relationship hinges on sex?
  Do I wish it played a more important part?
  A less important part?
  Is it perfect the way it is?

What do I bring to the relationship?

What do I expect my mate to bring to the relationship?
    Do I expect sacrifices?
    Do I make sacrifices for the relationship?

Could I progress faster without my mate?
    If the answer is yes,
    Would I rather progress slower *with* my mate?
    Towards what am I progressing?
    For which reason?

What am I without my mate (real or hoped for)?

Does having another to spend my life with give me a sense of security or of limitation—or both?
    Does it detract from the life I would like—or add to it?

Is our relationship built on a **need** for each other?

How much of my relationship (if there is one) is habit?
    How much do I concentrate on nurturing (as opposed to habit)?

How often does my relationship fill me with joy? And my partner?

When confronted in the relationship with a situation, am I:
    Forgiving

Positive (optimistic)
Negative (pessimistic)
Loving
Moody
Hurt
Supportive
Accepting
Manipulating

Who are the special people in my life?
    How does my partner compare/measure up to these people?
    What qualities do they have that I admire?
    What part do they play in my life?
    How do I (if I indeed do) nurture these relationships?
    With whom do I share my inner self?
    Do I share my inner self?

Who are the good listeners in my life?
    What qualities make a good listener?

Who understands me with few or no words?

Which qualities do I respect in others?
    How do these qualities mirror the qualities I desire for myself?

What meaning do these "discoveries" have for me?
    How will they affect my relationship with my partner?

Family Relations

How do I envisage a healthy family system functioning?

What role do I see myself playing within my family's structure?
    Am I happy with the dynamics of that role?

What do I need or want from my family members?
    How are my needs met?

Do I have to earn love to be a member of my family?
Am I rewarded for:
    My looks
    My intelligence
    My manners
    My generosity

Do I feel connected to any of my family members out of guilt?

Are my parents always emotionally available to me?

What painful or destructive patterns do I recognize in my family?
What strengths?

"What do **you** think?" is usually a trick question. How often have I been nailed for giving my opinion?

Can I think of any messages which my family relays to me?
    Are my responses predictable?
    Do they please me?
    Are they designed to "keep the peace?"
    Is it ever at the expense of **my** peace?

What choices do I need to make, regarding my family relations, to have them the way I would like them to be?

Business Relations

How would I define the role I play in the world in which I earn my livelihood.

Do I find what I do fulfilling?

Is the time spent in my business environment pleasurable?
    If not, what prevents it from being pleasurable?
    What could be done to make it pleasurable?

What is my primary reason for working?
    To make enough money to live.
    To be of service to mankind through my efforts.

Why do I do what I do?
    Because I love what I do.
    Because someone has got to do it.
    Because "it's a living."
    Because it was the only job available at the time.
    Because it's the family business—a tradition.
    Because it pleases my parents.

Is my first thought of what I can sell/do/perform for another individual or firm—or do I think of the money it will earn?

Do I see my business colleagues as competitors, friends, or money-making opportunities?

In business do I find myself on the defensive...
  Rarely
  Frequently
  Always
  Never

If a business venture/sale does not go through, do I find myself...
  Resentful
  Depressed
  Accepting
  Frustrated
  Motivated to try again

Am I always completely truthful in business?

Am I always completely fair?

If I had my choice, what would I be doing right now instead of the work in which I am engaged?

What is preventing me from doing it?

On Wealth

Am I as wealthy as I would like to be?

Do I consider wealth as:
  Money/securities/property.
  Friends.
  Health.
  or....

Do I define security as a financial cushion?
  Or the ability to make money through my own efforts?
  Or do I have faith that "the universe will always provide me with my needs?"

Do I believe that it is easier for a poor man to go through the eye of a needle?
  Do I want to go through the eye of a needle?

Do I believe that having money is a deterrent to spiritual growth?

Is having money a burden?

To which lengths would I go to make money?
   Work hard
   Take on more than one job
   Sell drugs or other illegal substances or articles
   Steal

Would I enter a relationship purely for the financial rewards?

Do I believe that money isn't everything—enough is enough and happiness comes first?

Does wealth equate with "things" in my life?

How would I describe wealth?
   Would I consider myself wealthy? and why?

Addictions

Definition: **Anything** which is chemically **or** psychologically a dependence. Another word for addiction is habit, although the word does not have the same connotation as addiction, they amount to the same. To test whether your habit can be considered an addiction, try dropping it for anywhere from a week to a month. If this causes you no anxiety, pain or discomfort, it is not an addiction.

Am I addicted to:
- Coffee or tea (with caffeine)
- Coffee or tea (de-caffeinated)
- Cigarettes (or other tobacco products)
- Chocolates (or other sugar loaded foods, e.g. candies, cakes, pies, cookies, etc.
- Meats or Fishes
- Alcohol (the big one)
- Drugs
    - Soft (marijuana, etc.)
    - Hard (heroin, cocaine, etc.)
- Aspirin, or other medications, prescribed by a doctor or not. This includes all pain killers.
- Tranquilizers.

Vitamins/minerals, and this includes all nutritional supplements including enzymes.
Digestive aids.
Chewing gum (bubble or plain)
Compulsive shopping
Movie going
Soft drinks (including diet sodas—no, especially diet sodas)
Laxatives
Any sexual practices, accepted as "normal" or otherwise
TV viewing
Jogging/running
Cleaning (Harriet Craig syndrome)
    Do I feel soiled by something
    Is something out of order in my life
Gambling
Weight lifting
Other obsessive behaviors
Anything else not named here?

On Health and Healing

From where do I believe healing comes?
    The doctor
    The hospital
    Drugs
    Medication
    Herbs
    Other

What are my feelings about health insurance?
    Does it give me a feeling of security?
    Am I expecting to collect on my health insurance?

What is **my** role in maintaining health?
    How am I playing my role
    Do I wait for my doctor to tell me what to do?
    What part of my life do I devote to
        preventive measures?
            What are they?
    If I knew for certain that drastic changes in my
        lifestyle were necessary for my perfect health—
        would I make the changes?
    If I knew for certain that drastic changes in my

lifestyle were necessary to prevent certain death if they were to continue—would I make the changes?

Am I aware of anything I do which does not enhance my health?
    Do I smoke?
    Do I drink alcohol? Soda pops? Diet sodas?
    Does my nutritional program leave something to be desired?
    Do I exercise sufficiently?
    Do I use drugs (medical or recreational)?
    Am I judgmental?
    Is my stress level high?
    Is my attitude acceptable? (or accepting?)
    Am I happy with my hygiene, inner and outer?

How many sore throats, colds, influenza bouts do I entertain each year?
    What have I noticed precedes each bout?

Do I suffer from headaches?
Do I have any muscular aches or pains on a regular basis?
    Exactly where are these located?

Do I enjoy being sick?
Do I enjoy being healthy?
What percentage of my life do I allow for each?

How do I feel when people around me become sick?
    Sympathetic
    Impatient
    Resentful
    Supportive
    Couldn't care less—that's their trip

Mental Health

What boundaries do I place around mental health?
Which boundaries are crossed to reach mental illness?
If "reality" entered into any of my boundaries—what are the boundaries of reality—what is real and what is unreal?

Do I come from a mentally healthy family?

On Sexuality

Do I consider my sexual practices fulfilling?
  Were they better in times past?
  Do I anticipate a positive change in the future?
  Am I frigid/abstaining?

What is the first sexual experience I can remember?
  Was it with a member of my own family?
  Was it a pleasurable experience?
  Was it a member of my own sex?
  What did I think about it at the time,
  Immediately afterwards,
  Much later upon retrospection?

Do I have any sexual fantasies?
  Have I lived them (played them out)?
Do I indulge (have I ever indulged) in auto-eroticism
  (masturbation)
    What goes on in my mind at these times?
  Have I ever played out fantasies in real life?
  Do I plan to one day if I haven't already?
  If the fantasy is of a remembered experience, will I
    repeat the experience?

Have I ever had intercourse with a member of my own sex?
> Once
> A couple of times
> Frequently

If I consider myself homosexual, have I ever had a sexual encounter with the opposite sex?
> Was it pleasurable?
> Will I repeat the experience?
> Do I consider myself bi-sexual?

Do I believe that sexual intercourse is:
Beautiful
Sacred
An experience shared with a special partner
An experience which when shared makes the partner special
Just an experience

Is sexual intercourse prior to marriage wrong, dirty?
Is sexual intercourse after marriage beautiful, wonderful exciting?
> Is it a marital duty?
> Is it an act purely for procreation of the species?
> Is it a favor in return for...?
>> Lifelong support
>> Momentary support
>> A mutually shared respite

Is it an integral part of life, a biological need, a way to experience joy through the senses?

Do I eagerly anticipate a sexual encounter?
- Do I dread one?
- Do I dream about one?
- Do I avoid one?

If in a marriage or a one on one relationship:

Is sex with my partner everything I dreamed it could be?

Is it frequent enough?

Does he/she require more frequent intercourse than I care for?

Is sex with my partner less pleasurable than I would like?

Is it too frequent?

When having intercourse with my mate, do I fantasize about another?

Have I ever had or thought of having a sexual encounter/relationship with one other than my mate?

How does my mate feel about intercourse with me?
How could intercourse with my mate be made more pleasurable?

Have my sexual fantasies ever been as exciting in
 a real life situation as they have been in
  my imagination?
 Have they ever been surpassed?

On Death and Dying

One thing in life is inevitable: if one is born, one day he will die. It is the lot of everyone. Is this true? or....

Do I think that I can escape death?

Taking into account **all** the ramifications (and thinking very carefully about them), would I choose to live forever?

Do I fear death?

What, if anything, do I fear about death?

We are told that the soul is immortal. What do I think the soul is? If it is immortal, where does it go after the body dies?

What do I believe happens when one dies? Do I **know** this? Do I believe anyone who tells me that **they** know? If so, why do I accept another's explanations?

Do I buy into the theory that there is a heaven, purgatory, and hell?

Do I fear punishment for sins committed during my lifetime?
> Of what am I guilty?
> Who has found me guilty?
> Who has passed sentence on me?
> Who will execute the punishment?

What are my feelings when someone close to me dies?

What are my feelings towards someone I know who "loses" to death someone they know and love?
> Does it embarrass me?
> Do I comfort them? How? What mundane platitudes do I mouth, if any?

What is my attitude toward funeral services? Cremation? Suicide?

Imagining myself at the end of this life span—am I happy with what I have done during my lifetime?
> What would I have done differently if I am not completely happy with what I perceive?
> What is preventing me from doing what would make me happy with my achievements during this lifetime?

What steps do I need to take to overcome the blocks which are preventing me from expressing what would make me happy with my life in retrospect at the time of leaving it?

Am I counting on another lifetime beyond this one to do what I am unable to do in this one?

What epitaph would I like to see on my tombstone—that is providing I or my loved ones opt for a grave with a tombstone?

Reincarnation—Other Lives

Do I believe that reincarnation is a fact? At least
   a possibility?
(If my answer to each part of the question is,
   "Without a doubt, **no**," I will read no farther
   but continue to the next chapter. However, if on
   future readings of the book I get an "It's a
   possiblity," then I shall read on.)

Have I had a past memory?

Is there a nation, civilization, or race of people
   with whom I feel a very close attraction? Affinity?
   Sympathy?

Is there one with whom I feel a total antipathy?
   Revulsion?

Is there a pattern in my life (a cycle of events)
   which repeats itself despite anything I may do to
   avoid it?

What can I think of—real or imagined—that could
   possibly justify my experiencing this "chain of

events." This constantly recurring reaction, this slipping into such a predictable behavior pattern?

Which dreams, or daydreams, can I remember in which I portray a character other than my present self, but whom I recognize so well?

Which period in history, past or future, do I feel strongly attracted to?

Which period in history strongly repels me, gives me a feeling a horror or dread?

What kind of life could I conjure up which would act as a see-saw or balance to the one in which I am presently involved?

God, Saints, and Devils

What is my own, **very specific** personal concept of God (not what I have been taught by rote, and not what I have been told or have read but what I truly believe?)

What do I feel were the specific roles on earth of:
  Jesus
  The Virgin Mary
  Moses
  Buddha
  Krishna
  Lao-tse
  Confucius

  Karl Marx
  Abraham Lincoln
  Hitler
  Mohammed

Do I believe that there are angels?
  How would I define an angel, and their role in the scheme of things.

Do I believe that everyone has his/her own
   guardian angel?

How do I believe a saint becomes a saint?
   What is the role of a saint in his/her lifetime?
   After his/her death?
   Does the saint have a choice about their role?
   Do I know any [potential] saints?

What (or who) do I believe is the devil? Satan?
   Can I remember experiencing any manifestation
      of the devil?
   Do I fear a confrontation with the devil?
   How would I protect myself from the devil if he
      indeed does exist?

Do I believe that people who have died return to
   earth in the form of ghosts? Use mediums to
   communicate with those still alive?
      If yes, does this scare me or comfort me?
      If it scares me, of what am I afraid?
      If it comforts me, how and why?

Do I believe that I can contact God in church
   easier than I can elsewhere?
      Do I go to church with any regularity?
      If no, do I wish that I did?
      If yes, do I wish that I didn't have to, or
         am I glad that I do?

What do I believe is a church's main function?

How effective do I believe prayer to be?
   How does prayer work?

Jesus healed the sick—do I believe that the same healing can be accomplished today?
   If yes, how do I believe spiritual healing works?
   If one person can heal spiritually, can others?
   What would prevent me from performing healings?

What exactly do I believe meditation is?
   Do I practice it?
   If yes, do I find it beneficial?
      In what way?
   If no, do I think it could benefit me if I did?
   If yes, what is preventing me from practicing meditation?

Universal Philosophy

Do I believe that everything in the world is pre-ordained, that it follows a pattern?
> Is this belief comforting or disturbing?
> If I accepted this belief as truth, how would it change my life as it is now?

Do I believe that nothing in the world is fixed, that I make everything happen as it happens?
> Or do I believe that circumstances make things happen?
> If I accepted this belief as truth, how would it change my life as it is now?

Am I sitting on the fence, believing that certain things are preordained or fixed in the path of inevitability, but that I can control other factors in my life?
> How much of my life do I actually control?
> What would happen if I gave up control over these "controllable" facets of my life?
> Or all of it?
> If I don't have control over my life, who or

what do I believe actually does?
Am I happier when I am in control?
Am I happier when I give up control entirely—
can I give up control entirely?

Do I believe in moderation in all things? Or am
I an extremist—doing whatever I do with such zeal
and enthusiasm that it often burns out like
a meteor?

If what I do with such zeal and enthusiasm lasts,
do I believe that it is an obsession? Or a habit
pattern? Or even a rut?

Does anything or anyone have control over me?

Do I believe that a person can be possessed?
Define possession.

> Am I overweight (too much food or lack of
>   exercise or both)?
> Do I smoke?
> Am I an inveterate gambler?
> Do I drink alcohol as a social drinker? More?
>
> Do I require medication?
>   Do I take it regularly? Constantly?
>
> Am I in a relationship that consumes me?
>   If not, do I want to be?

Does my happiness depend on **anything** outside of myself?

Do I believe I must be about my father's business?
What **is** my father's business?
Am I performing my father's business?

Is my present a victim of my past?

If it is, does that make my future a victim of my "now?" Where is the point of power to be happy?

Exploring the "us and them" consciousness, on what level do I think of people as "us and them"?

Intergalactic:	Us and the Extra-Terrestrials?
International:	Us and the Russians (or other nations)? This is evident at the Olympic games.
National:	Us and those in other states?
Statewide:	Us and those from other cities?
College Level:	Our school against their school?
Religions:	Us and those heathens (or hell-bent, misguided souls, or those religious fanatics)?
Social:	Us and Them (pure and simple)?

Economic: Us and them (with pity in the voice—
for either direction)?
Racial: Us and them?
Hippy versus the Establishment?
The American Medical Association versus alternative healing methods?
Rival businesses?
Us and those neighbors?
Us and the other people bordering our space?

Who do I believe wrote the bible?
   By whom was it updated/revised?
   Are there are any other versions?
   Who was the author of the scrolls discovered at Nag Hammadi? The Dead Sea Scrolls?
   Has the author of the bible written any other books before or since the bible?
     If so, what are their titles?
        Are there any other communications/papers/essays?

Dreams

Do I remember my dreams?

Do I never remember dreaming?
    Do I awaken with feelings, even if I never remember the dream which gives rise to the feeling?

Are there any past dreams (or nightmares) which I remember vividly?
    How often have they occurred for me to remember that vividly?
    Was it a prophetic dream? Was the prophesy fulfilled?
        If not, need I act upon it? Will I act upon it?

Do I believe that dreams are merely the result of what we had for dinner?

Or, do I believe that dreams are messages from the inner self?

What is the most important part of the dreams to interpret?

THE CRUCIAL QUESTIONS

    The feeling it leaves me with
    The locale of the dream
    The situation
    The people in the dream

How might I interpret:
    A car, a bus, a ship, a train (or other vehicle)
    Death
    An accident

A fortuitous happening (like winning a sweepstakes)

Attitudinal Responses

Am I a "live wire" as far as reactions are concerned? Do I react instantaneously or does a situation need to take time to mature within me before I react?

Am I spontaneous—responding to instincts?

Do I anticipate all (or most) possible occurrences?

Do I "rehearse" my reactions well ahead of time, making sure that I have all my bases covered?

How would I react to:
    Attempted rape
    Discovering I have been burglarized
    Hearing of a major catastrophe
    A minor catastrophe
    Arriving home to find a surprise party awaiting me
    Being given an unexpected gift
    A compliment

What would my instinctive reaction be if:
    All the lights went out and I was in total darkness
    I find myself on a very high precipice
    I am threatened by a total stranger...

In a public place with people around
   In a secluded place where no one is nearby

I discover that I have been overcharged or shortchanged?

How would I react if I came home and found my spouse (or live-in mate) in bed with another?
   Would I accept it with a "laissez faire" attitude?
   Would I be angry?
   Would I be forgiving?
      After laying a guilt trip, or before?
   Would I turn around, creep out, and...
      Burn
      Cry
      Get drunk
      Find myself someone with whom I could be unfaithful?
   Would I join them?

What would my reaction be if I made a bid for a contract only to discover that I had been outbid by $100?
   Would I want to kick myself?
   Would I say, "Oh well! I guess that's the game?"
   Would I go out and do something to take my mind off it?

What would my reaction be if a car hit my car while
 driving (nothing serious, just a fender bender)?
  If it were a careful older driver?
  One driving while under the influence of alcohol?
What would my reaction be if **I** hit a car, and I
 knew it was my fault?
If it were **not** my fault?

What would my instinctive response be if I were to
 enter someone's front yard and was confronted by
 a large, barking dog whose tail was **not** wagging?

How would I react if I went to the doctor for a
 routine medical check-up and was told that I had
 an inoperable condition and that I only had three
 months to live?
  Would I accept it—go home and wait to die?
  Would I accept it, put my house in order, and prepare
   for death?
  Would I cry and deny it?
  Would I get second, third or fourth opinions?
  Would I seek alternative medical services?
  Would I seek a spiritual healing?
  Would I simply refuse to believe it?

If I am a sexually active adult: How would I react to
 hearing that someone with whom I had been sexually
 involved within the past two years has AIDS?

Beliefs, Programs and Mundanities

Which of these expressions do I use?
  Excuse me for living.
  He/she/it is a pain in the butt—pain in the neck—just a pain.
  He/she/it drains me. I feel drained.
  I am sick and tired of....
  I am just dying to...
  I am terrified that...
  Excuse me...
  I am afraid that...
  So sorry...sorry

With which of these expressions/superstitions have I been programmed.
    A stitch in time saves nine.
    He who hesitates is lost.
    Look before you leap.
    It's water under the bridge.
    Don't cry over spilt milk.
    When in Rome...do as the Romans do.

Judge not lest ye be judged.
Step on a crack, break your mother's back.
Get caught in the rain—you'll catch a cold.
Walking under a ladder brings bad luck.
Don't let a black cat cross your path.
Beware of Friday the 13th.
Eat the last (something) on the plate and you'll end up an old maid.
Sing before breakfast—cry before supper.
Spill salt—throw some over your left shoulder to ward off ill-luck.
Knock on wood.

Futures

Changing one's parameters/perimeters.

What choices do I need to make in my life to have it the way I would like it to be?

Have I resolved my birth trauma—if there was a need to forgive my parents, have I forgiven them?

Am I at peace with my childhood?

Am I expressing my personal image to my complete satisfaction?

Are my relations with my family in total harmony?

Is my relationship with my partner balanced to my satisfaction?

Is my attitude towards my business/work/profession at a point where I am happy?

Have I come to grips with those lifestyles/habits which tend to control/possess me?

Are my reactions less volatile? Is my balance of spontaneity to my liking?

Do I feel financially secure?

Am I comfortable with my inner teachings/intuition?

Have I come to grips with my dreams? Do I work with them instead of ignoring them?

Am I resolved with the inevitability of death—has my attitude towards it been resolved?

Am I listening to what I say (and think) realizing that I can program myself to believe things at a deeper level than I would choose to believe consciously?

What have I left undone which I really need to do to allow me to be totally peaceful?

Epilogue

I struggled long and hard about writing an epilogue. First and foremost, I did not want to influence or color any of the discoveries which you had made. And then, maybe I did not want to share my innermost beliefs or personal truisms. But, I felt that I owed my readers who had travelled this far with me a glimpse of my belief structure, bearing in mind that it is just that—a belief structure. Every book should have a beginning and an end if it is to leave its readers satisfied. Questions which arise need to be resolved—and heaven knows, this book has more than its share of questions. This epilogue then is my attempt to add the finishing touch, the icing on the cake, the cherry on the sundae.

Having worked with the questions, can you now see the importance of asking the right question to find the right answer? Have you noticed that our lives are filled with unfinished sentences; unfinished thoughts; incomplete statements? Perhaps to complete the statement would give us an insight which we need for enlightenment. Many times we feel that we are on the brink of discovery (discovery of what?), on the brink of knowing

(knowing what?). Put a name to it and we have it. Fears: to name our fear is to claim it, to bring it into the light where it can be intelligently dealt with to the point where it is no longer a fear. Consider these expressions which we sometimes encounter: "The only safe place to be...." safe from what? "Our protection, Lord, is in thee...." protection from what? One of my favorites is, "If only I were free...." free **from** what or free to **do** what?

When we see what is binding us and holding us to or from something, we often find that the knots are illusions and that we **are** free, and it is this freedom to enter the realm of the unknown which is feared. If we could enter the unknown future unfettered by past experiences, memories, programming, would we be less fearful? We have lived all our lives with boundaries, limitations, and the perimeters of do's and don'ts which have formed our personalities from birth. Programming is performed by ourselves through parents, relatives, guardians, friends, teachers—anyone we allow—indeed, by life (or the illusion of life) itself. Our fear then is not really of **not** being free, for this is a known condition. As the old saying goes: better a devil you know than a devil you don't know (how about no devil at all?). The unknown condition **is** freedom...from the self-inflicted boundaries...to the universality of **being**. This is what we fear, this is what we "protect" ourselves from. So let us be honest—we don't really want freedom, we want the status quo which is a condition of being bound and being able to bemoan the fact that we are not free.

The "if only's" are our conflicts. Conflicts are what are needed to keep us in the earth plane—the time/space continuum. Without the duality of conflict, the game of life is not quite the same. Open our eyes, the game is over, and we need to start another one. It is like the game of hide and seek, when the hidden is discovered, with much laughter and excitement, it is time to choose another to hide so that the game can start over again—or to play another game—or to rest from playing games, although that is very difficult. To interact with the universe, we need to have a mask, a personality through which to communicate. Put on the mask, take off the mask...we need a character through which to interact, and so we create the character. The more outrageous the character, the more daredevilish the deed, the more exciting the script we write from moment to moment.

When Gertrude Stein wrote "a rose is a rose is a rose" perhaps she saw the game within the games...the illusion of movement. The French have a saying: The more something changes, the more it remains the same. Or as the English version states it: It is not so much one thing after another, as it is the same thing over and over again. If we look at our "changes" we will see not changes so much as cycles, each one thinly disguised to fool us into thinking that we are trying something new. If we delve into our patterns (hates, fears, resentments—even loves, emotions and relationships) we will see the cycles. Every so often something truly outrageous happens which makes everyone gasp, something which might bring a tear to the eye or jerk the emotions to the maximum. Why have we written this into the script? What are we saying with this action?

    The personality does not give up easily, its survival mechanism knows all the tricks. The games it can play are inexhaustible. One of its favorite games is the "yes...but" game. Point out a *faiblesse* and the personality will say "YES...BUT...." One game which helps break the cycle of experience that we play (yes, it is another game) is the "Ah, so" game. This is another version of the "Thank you, Father" game. It is acceptance, rather than the "Why me?" game. The "why me game" has been lessened in impact by the answer "who else?" Who would we rather have in the situation in which we find ourselves? How could we want another to be in the situation we are in if it is not pleasant? Why **are** we in the position in which we find ourselves? What is that we say?

We don't know why were are in the position we are in? Whose fault is it? Whom can we blame—WHAT will we blame? Put anything at all outside ourselves in charge (or to carry the blame) and we are possessed by an outside force. Possession is by **anything** which controls us against our will. But even that is an illusion as we discover the oneness of all being. That which we give power over us is of our own making. So really we are possessed by ourselves, or by our own creation.

What limits are there to the number of games we will play? Creativity can be measured by the situations which we can create to amuse ourselves and others—for by being, we teach. What then do we wish to teach, what then will we be? If we accept the "being" it is one game, if we don't accept the "being," it is another—until we decide to stop playing. Will we die, not with a bang, but a whimper? Or will we choose something spectacular? How long can we maintain the novelty of our script, for in this lies fame, immortality in the illusion. Look at Caesar, Jesus, Michelangelo, Da Vinci, Hitler, Buddha, I could go on and on. Our lives in the scheme of time are like so many ripples on a pond. The bigger the splash we make, the larger the ring of ripples and the longer they last. Come on, let's make a splash. After all is said and done, life is just something to do between birth and death.

Are there any questions which you feel would be meaningful which I have failed to include under the subject headings?

Are there any subject headings which you feel would be beneficial to explore that are not in this book?

If you are interested in group work? Please send your name, address and phone number and we will be pleased to put you in touch with other interested parties in your area.

Your comments are invited.

Lawrence M. Steinhart
c/o The Donning Company/Publishers
5659 Virginia Beach Boulevard
Norfolk, Va. 23502

Further Reading on Spiritua[l]

Edgar Cayce's secrets of BEAUTY THROUGH HEALTH

by Lawrence M. Steinhart

nd Physical Well Being

Lawrence M. Steinhart

From the international beauty authority a unique and timely assemblage of information channeled by the renowned psychic, Edgar Cayce, giving his most pertinent and comprehensive advice on all aspects of inner and outer beauty and health.

THE OUTER YOU
Practical yet inspired advice on care of the skin, hair, teeth, hands, feet, nails and eyes. Complete with formulas that can be made at home along with common sense remedies generally available without prescription.

THE INNER YOU
A complete guide to proper nutrition, exercise, diet, and massage.

THE TOTAL YOU
Unparalleled counsel on achieving inner peace through understanding reincarnation, dreams, the spiritual and astrological influences on your being and rejuvenation.

BEAUTY THROUGH HEALTH is an essential guide to beauty for the whole person, spiritual as well as physical.

THE
DONNING COMPANY
PUBLISHERS
NORFOLK/VIRGINIA BEACH
DISTRIBUTOR